A View of
Ourselves

David Ben Foster

BlueSky
PUBLISHING PARTNERS

Library of Congress Control Number: 2013908946
ISBN: 0989358313

BlueSky
PUBLISHING PARTNERS
ASSISTED SELF-PUBLISHING & MARKETING SERVICES

PO Box 1525, Medina, Ohio 44258
www.BlueSkyPublishingPartners.com

For information about custom editions, special sales, and premium corporate purchases, please contact BlueSky Publishing Partners at 855-721-1833.

Printed in the United States of America
Second Edition

Acknowledgements

To my wife Catherine, for I am lovingly appreciative of her encouragement, graciousness, and patience.

A View of
Ourselves

DEDICATION TO CATHERINE

There is no night so tender, as with you,

nor beauty as erotic, yet so fair.

The blossom of your smile I'll not eschew,

for pressed upon my mind, it's always there.

I've kissed the nectar from your luring lips

and sipped your cup of wine until imbibed.

My inhibitions wane as you eclipse

the memories, the unexplained, as did

your noble femininity, my love.

Deceptive friend was solace once beseeched;

now private time with you I'm jealous of.

You are the joy, the pinnacle I've reached.

You are the passion I possess, and more,

my Catherine, the woman I adore.

CONTENTS

AN INTERLUDE

Forget me not when I have passed away,

nor let my shadow fade from memory.

When blossoms paint the meadows bright in May,

please sing within your heart our melody;

for time cannot annul the joy we had,

nor steal as death appears has taken too.

And yes, there will be moments when you're glad—

before the lie that I've forsaken you,

with suddenness and frightfulness intrudes—

because I loved you more than life itself.

Deny the falsity which spawns these moods

remembering the things you've said yourself,

that life embraces both the flawed and whole,

and on each man and beast, exacts a toll.

Autumn Wine

I enjoy

drinking Autumn wine

listening to the colors of Fall,

rolling in velvet meadows, and

whispering to the grass.

Soon the sun will slip south,

the forest will sleep, and

washed-out stains will stir

in gusts of wintry air.

April rains smelling green, and

chills from Winter's repose

disappear in Spring's rebirth.

Days lengthen as evenings linger, but

shortly, well-born friends

find me unsuitable, for

I am happy most,

drinking Autumn wine.

Who's Next?

Earth breathed before

we appeared;

sustaining life,

often smiling on us.

Gifted;

powerful;

we indulged.

Unrestrained, ignoring the Voice,

breaching the trust,

we pollute,

spoil resources

destroy shore lines,

betraying our birthright.

UNDERSTANDING

The joys of life were crowded

with complexities

that left me unquiet.

I sought refuge in the Simple.

Now I slumber in her arms.

Prodigal's Dilemma

Seeking personal reprieve

I nightly walked in thought

of forbidden deserts.

Curiosity beckoned

inflaming my desire for merely

a taste of the un-partaken.

Drained from excess,

I wandered back

where now, I run quietly.

DESTINED

Deserted, and averted any prize,

I could not see tomorrow, even us.

neither head, nor heart could mask, disguise

what presumably was missed, and nonplus.

This paradox, this flux, and troubled mess

is cast, quite fixed for lonely souls of men.

My part, played once, is void of hope, I guess,

and lost, as a sage in a darkened den.

We can't pretend as though our love is right,

for if it was, this discourse wouldn't be.

Yet, shelter me, embrace me just tonight;

forget the past, this talk, these lies of me.

Allow today to pass, why press the grain?

For the present counts, nothing will remain.

WARM ILLUSIONS

I watched the moon, her ever measured lift,

rise slowly into the heavens colored blue.

Her mystery intriguing, as thoughts flew,

while pondering her beauty—evening's gift,

among eternal lights which ever shift.

I thought of life lent to me, years so few;

I then recalled her beams were borrowed too.

Reminded of the memories which drift

like fantasies of happiness that pass,

when sanity of life would seem to flee.

These shapeless cyclic thoughts of gold and brass,

At times emerge abruptly, and I'm free.

Like morning shadows through a window glass,

They fade into the light, again I'm me.

Honesty

If memory is the wisp of thought

which was conjured in deceit,

then references that we possess

are omens of defeat.

And the gnawing cancer hidden within

consumes the self by and by,

for thoughts today are unable to quench the fire,

nor excise the pseudo high.

Why then do we knowingly attempt

to mask our inventive past,

when confession is the soul's release?

Choice?

Born in mire

reared in the streets.

Privacy, a darkened alley

happiness, my Dad's smile

comfort, my Mom's touch.

Living in the shadows

but without you, I'll die unnoticed.

EARTHEN VESSELS

While sipping mortal wine,

serious smiles appeared;

then laughter echoed

in shallow hearts.

Music filled the theater, as

thespians spoke to smoke-like forms;

dancers celebrated Time;

then suddenly everyone applauded,

as though excited by something real.

Midnight

Pure happiness eludes the best of men.

Elusiveness: the trait of the portent;

its momentary lapse allures and then

she leaves her mark of disillusionment.

Misfortune cleaves to me, and woe befits;

the two befriend and ever spoil my hope,

and subsequently all my life unfits.

Thus, blinded by this disarray, I grope

for inquiring truth that confronts, and acts

as though it tends to undermine my thought.

My weary soul inflames; my blood reacts

Sending me drifting in the land of Naught.

At times I wish that God would end this play.

This actor's done; I've lost the fun today.

THE GRASS IS GREEN AGAIN

Blades of green sparkle in dew;

reflections flicker on the gravestone as

warm rays of sun blink

through breeze-blown leaves.

She gave, expecting little.

I never understood the flare for life

she possessed.

Strange?

The morning chill is gone,

and the grass is green again.

Covetousness

The wish for carnality causes

the flame of desire to lick

feverishly at its object.

So it was with him—requiring more.

Sheds continued to burst with fruits;

he reaped solely through efforts of others.

Larger barns were erected and seasons

gave with little rest—even the elements

seemed to obey.

"A god is never satisfied," he mused

as death swallowed him.

Beloved

It's not the way you smile,

nor is it your loving touch;

but the loving life you give to mine.

It's not because you bridged our space,

nor carried me in love;

but the oneness you have made of us.

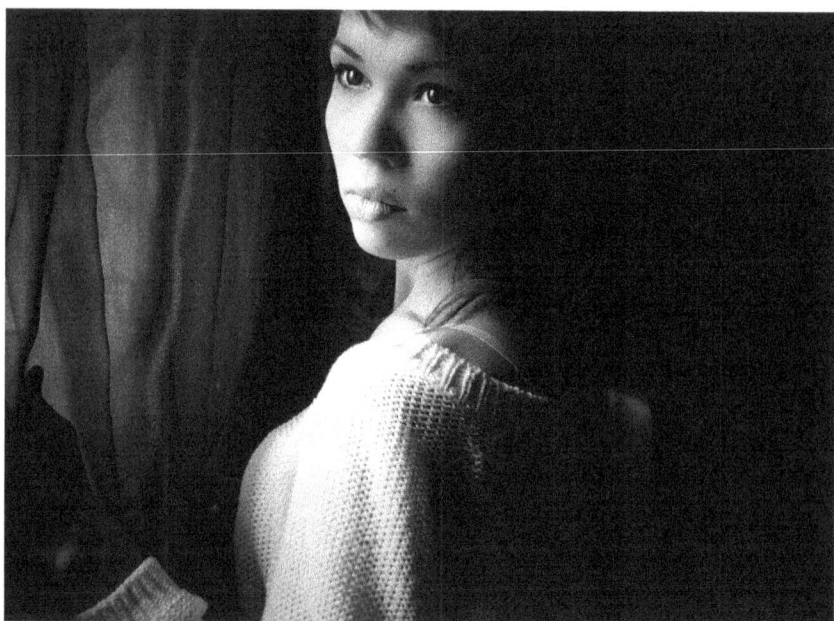

DAUGHTER

The journey we will share is one of toil,

but not the common kind man must endure.

This added burden hopefully won't spoil

the joyfulness, your aspirations pure.

An explanation of this dreary view

begins before we knew we wanted you;

and years before the winds of passion blew,

Inviting music, out of which love grew,

impatience birthed what lies did formulate,

that soon had turned to question and regret.

Redress was gone, and queries much too late,

for social flaws as this, breed human debt.

And those drawn in by choice, or ones like you,

must bear this burden of your parents too.

Prophets

Silhouettes speak in frosted air;

faceless profiles of doom

always inciting others,

predicting the present,

ever circling,

unaware of the own.

Risks

Enter the forbidden

Discover the concealed

Pursue your love

Escape—the stage is guarded

by the curtain of dusk.

Mainstream

We all live in our

own back yard

staring at fences

someone else built;

we defend what

probably won't endure;

hoping to change

what will anyway.

DEPLETING

I've often wondered, often felt the urge

to spar with fate, or tempt the sting of death.

Inventive thoughts incite the blood to surge;

awakened heart responds to rapid breath;

and soon I'm lost, delivered from the real.

This fulsome lure, this attitude of dare

has not appeased, nor changed the way I feel;

for never have my efforts gained a share.

So whether here or there, it's just the same—

a man that's sure to win, alas to lose.

It's merely life, there's no appointing blame,

but when the Reaper calls, I'll leave the blues;

I'll leave behind the shining world for those

who love, and blindly trek where nothing grows.

IDENTITY

Knowing the foreboding call,

ignoring voices,

she grasped my hand

pointing toward tomorrow;

Assuring that we will be.

Dawn

She walked in the early sun

her feet wet with dew; and

hopes of conquering in her breast.

The day passed;

the meadows will miss her.

ATHANASIA

Winging through the wind—

a word of hope in unheard sounds

which live in mysteries,

couched in the currents

of the invisible arms of the wind.

Will we ever embrace these secrets,

knowing as God knows,

that life exists before we see it?

An arcane image leaves trails of

warm elements wherever it gives

granting us its endlessness.

In this flux of opposites,

fears fizzle and burn out

when silence speaks unspeakable wisdom.

Deaf ears strain, hearing the heart, but

missing the music of Eternity's concert.

STRESS

The lights go out, and I'm alone again.

This solace rends my thoughts to parallels:

the one seductively attracts the brain;

the other repulsively attempts spells.

I waver like a double-minded man:

the wrong—the right, as primitive as life.

This struggle blazes on as though its span

would have no end; as with a jagged knife,

I'm ripped, left scared by fate's unmasked design.

Reprieve comes slowly with the morning light,

and to this calming dawn I soon resign.

Rejuvenation quells these dreams of fright

that linger 'til ascending sun appears,

and for that moment, removes my fears.

Assassins

Murders—scarring the world;

moving on transparent layers of slime,

spewing self-proclaimed justice,

slaying as though each time closer

to global cleansing.

These private executioners

prohibit wars to cease,

believing their nightmare; and

crazed by madness.

Hate—their passion;

vengeance—their excuse.

Sovereigns

Sprinkling, splashing everywhere,

inexhaustibly,

we monarchs of nothing

pretend to understand,

asking in vain,

"Where is God?"

Her Smile

She wears the night as though it was her own.

In subtle gestures, swings her head and hips,

and walks the boulevard in search of bone

to satisfy the hate her heart now grips.

Tonight she'll tease and please another man

without the slightest hint of love or care.

Emotions, just as foreign to her pain,

as numb as life was never to be fair.

The precious gold adorns her slenderness,

mere tokens of the price she's paid, and still,

her path is paved with fear and bitterness.

Her shallow laughter haunts and leaves a chill.

The lies, the shame, will ever be the same.

We know her smile, but never know her name.

He Looked Familiar

Somewhere on Sunday, there was a man

searching intently, almost frantically,

for paths of righteousness;

the ones unmistakably pure.

Finding everything he hadn't sought,

unjustly burdened as equity eluded him,

he succumbed to anguish.

Mistake

If suffering should be the salt in life,

then daughter dear, I've set you up for sure:

unnecessary pain and anxious strife

with questions, ever questions, like a blur

before your searching eyes so sadly down.

Your mother too, knows well my silent moods,

and wonders what's behind my thinking frown.

Still I believe within her heart she broods,

"He contemplates the day he'll slip away."

But I've no plan to leave my loves behind.

Decisions that I've made before today

were never meant to paint your world unkind.

This compromise was not with you in view;

I'm sorry for your mother, and for you.

Excursions

The sun ignites the gulf

sinking slowly into a motionless sea

as though her lambent flame

too hot to bear.

Day creatures, invited by night

are excused of burdens.

Thoughts drift to a better day

as the warm beach turns cold.

CITY SKYLINE

Softly chiseled against the night,

a silhouette of collective life.

Inviting are the shadows,

reflections of hope.

But then, we see what we need.

SOME BY WILL

I don't hear the same music;

I'm unable to understand tomorrow;

but I'm here today:

food

drink

a cardboard box.

Homeless?

I have a friend

Slipping Into No One

Evolving, revolving in acid time;

the future looks traumatically unfit,

but I'm the man who's guilty of the crime,

this misdeed now entwines, impedes my wit.

My stomach tells me daily of this breach,

and although busy passing moments here

in sweat, I'm not so far my mind can't reach

uncertainty; giving more than, I fear,

than I get, regardless of asserted will.

All compromise have blurred, deceive my view;

eccentricities—muted by a pill.

And then one day I'll no longer be blue.

Lonely days seem to pass in spite of me;

they'll waste away, but so will I you see.

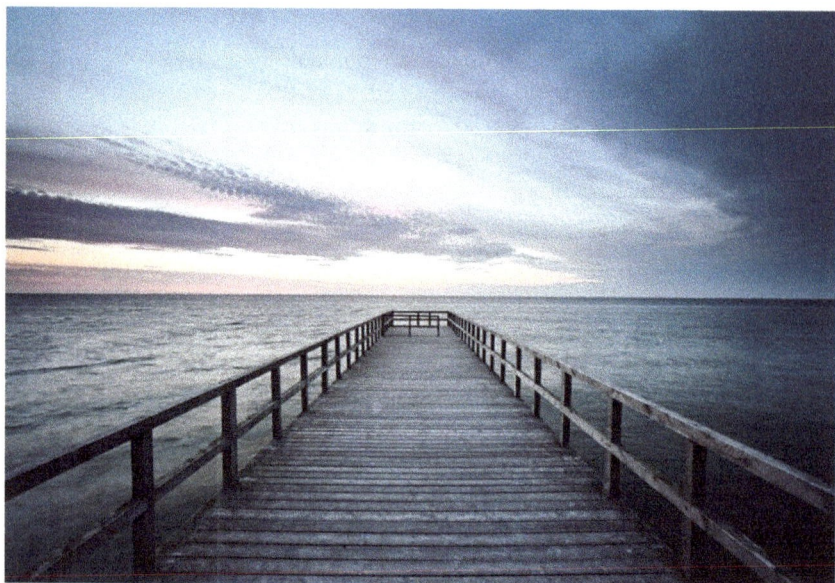

REFLECTIONS

Flesh is not a prison.

Man—where Epiphanies of truth

flicker in darkness;

where the current of ambivalence,

known as being,

perceives rays of reality

as flashes from a single Source.

Many fumble in these lights,

choosing to falter,

denying that life perpetually

entreats rebirth

uncertain that striving is worth the pain.

To Hemingway

Though life is not a hedonistic play,

it surely is theatrical in form

where cruel games of love are seen each day;

where no one wins, but dismal in the norm.

All good is sullied by some blight,

and attitudes twist truth with bias thought.

I never measure up—I thought I might,

so I've resigned to bend as life has taught,

for happiness is someone else's joy.

I've moved from mess to mess with hopeful zeal,

beginning when an enterprising boy.

One day when God will judge, reveal with zeal,

what parents created in hidden ploy,

fashioning men quite able to destroy.

Excessive

The sigh of nature;

the cry for life.

Green fading into dust,

blue washing poison to the shore,

grey turning to rust;

unimaginable yesterday, and

unforeseen this morning.

Wisdom begs to be heard.

PROBATION PASSED

One morning sullen smiles

will quiet unhappy laughter.

The carnal stage will vanish

as though it had never existed;

the eternal gulf will widen

as the separation in born,

and restlessly, irrevocably trapped,

they will chase, in black air,

desires unattainable.

The days of discipline have waned, as heart;

and all is tainted with untruth, it seems.

A selfish loyalty prevails, impart

because mere talk of dauntlessness, like schemes,

invented to portray what couldn't be;

obscures the truth and ruefully deceives.

It's this pathetic state man boosts as free

while time rebukes and mocks, the dull mind cleaves:

perhaps tomorrow, the answer, so they muse;

but seasons change and rearrange the age.

A will infers a choice that we misuse,

and corresponding consequence is rage:

allegiance to veracity and nerve;

but seldom conscience proves what we deserve.

THE MORNING SENTENCE

He sits silently in the shadow;

tears wet the cold grey cement

between his shackled feet.

Ideas of nothingness grip his mind,

and fear charges his blood.

Calmly a voice questions,

"Is there anything I can give you?"

His white swollen face peers up,

"Give me tomorrow."

OPIATES

Trapped in a bubble—

pink shadows in green air;

music begging to be touched;

suddenly swallowed by strange voices

while tasting the cooled sun—

we dance in mud.

Unmasked

Prejudice, once spoken

no longer walks as a friend.

Listen to the rhythm of the times:

songs sung off-key

by chattering pawns

who dance in dust.

Bigotry betrays.

QUESTIONABLE

Uncertainty—an element of life,

the spoiler of the best intentions, goals;

the callous thief of dreams for hopeless souls;

the unsuspected courier of strife—

is more than merely happenstance or fate.

Its brazen calculation goads the best,

forbidding even saints a lengthy rest;

inventing ways to stir the heart to hate;

and yet, envision life, if void of chance

with stagnant minds, fixed spirits never free;

where men exist without the need to glance

within themselves for greater strengths to be

a person other than who they are—perchance,

who could, by resolve, shape their destiny.

PROCURERS

Refuse enticement to whoredom.

Sacrificing truth

is to burn integrity

on a fallacious altar of compromise.

Cry

choices are being made for you—

regulation, legislation

like shimmering light on a polluted river

giving lip service to the arts

to the impoverished, to the environment;

prevarications in the name of significance

like self-serving gods above the created.

Behind oak doors in white fortifications

their laughter mocks;

you are the social security number

they intend to seduce

they are tenacious.

Demand

accountability to this affront

strengthen your resolve

cross your legs to their threat of rape.

PROVIDED

In my breast a torment stirred,

winds of unknown origin.

Secretly I fought to quell

their rending, painful courses;

sought to reprieve in masquerade.

Deep in the sterile night

my barren soul remained afraid

of each day's unforgiving light.

Anger held life in line;

the truth—instability.

Mirrored thoughts of whose design?

Havoc—insecurity,

as the Psalmist, I questioned why

God's Heaven remained silent;

why He would pass by

knowing what I knew He saw,

terrifying things done to me.

Would life pass before I

could taste delight with a lover?

Life was mine to please, or taunt

I thought as I considered death.

My sightless will was unable to select

a place to begin anew

for overwhelming weight paralyzed

my soul like the toe of my shoe crushes a cigarette.

Futility, yes, I believed that God would

release this damaging fear;

miraculously wash away my yesterday

and embrace me.

Quietude and solitude—friends

of comfort and calm,

loving me as I desired of God.

At least, that's what I had been told.

Where was He when I was small,

when alone, sobbing alone, after

the worst kind of robbery?

While contemplating my demise,

anger firmly at my side,

an un-thought flash widened my eyes,

after which I tried to hide:

"Who gave anger to survive,

the fury to live?"

Although summer was late in returning,

and the past had forever fixed itself,

God had refashioned me.

For those who defraud the young

twisting trust into disgrace

leaving them enraged,

it is the anger that sustains, but returns them.

Today I move along quietly,

conceivably as He initially had calculated.

INDIFFERENCE

Winter waves break at the door

spraying white mists against windows frosted.

Mornings find us wading in crusted swells,

goading puffs of wind at our backs.

The elements have their obligations.

BETRAYAL

Betrayal—

intentions gone awry

fidelity compromised,

a self-destructive predicament.

Reason lied.

Penance, never enough;

love stained.

Clothed in humility,

forgiveness remains

the paradox.

Hear Me?

I know,

Like Able, my blood cries out from discolored ground

Again the victim passes quietly from view, but

the murderer couldn't change who I was,

yet violently robbed who I was to become.

My children will live in doubt

suffocated by anger and unanswered questions,

plagued by the incomprehensible act upon me.

My parents weep for justice

as loss cloaks them in abandonment.

My siblings think "vengeance,"

then cup their nervous hands over quivering mouths,

muffling arguments of hate, as reason struggles to be heard.

Who hears me?

Everyone born to love life,

who shares it with others, as we once had,

touching, as we will again.

Our joy will mingle, laugh, and sing without a breach

or bereavement when you come to me.

Comfort, my comfort I leave you.

www.ingramcontent.com/pod-product-compliance
Lightning Source LLC
Chambersburg PA
CBHW060744100426
42813CB00032B/3392/J